Teach Me...™
Everyday
FRENCH
Volume 1

Written by Judy Mahoney
Illustrated by Patrick Girouard

Technology is changing our world. Far away exotic places have literally become neighbors. We belong to a global community and our children are becoming "global kids." Comparing and understanding different languages and cultures is more vital than ever! Additionally, learning a foreign language reinforces a child's overall education. Early childhood is the optimal time for children to learn a second language, and the Teach Me Everyday Language Series is a practical and inspiring way to teach them. Through story and song, each book and audio encourages them to listen, speak, read and write in a foreign language.

Today's "global kids" hold tomorrow's world in their hands. So when it comes to learning a new language, don't be surprised when they say, "teach me!"

French is spoken in many countries around the world, not just in France. Like Spanish, it is one of the Romance languages. It is also the official language of Canada, as well as the United Nations. French-speaking countries and regions within them have their own dialects. All French nouns have a gender which means the article preceding the noun indicates masculine or feminine as well as singular or plural.

Teach Me Everyday French
Volume One
ISBN 13: 978-1-59972-101-9
Library of Congress PCN: 2008902654

Copyright © 2008 by Teach Me Tapes, Inc.
6016 Blue Circle Drive, Minnetonka, MN 55343
www.teachmetapes.com

Book Design by Design Lab, Northfield, MN

10 9 8 7 6 5 4 3 2

INDEX & SONG LIST

Plus nous sommes ensemble
Plus nous sommes ensemble, ensemble, ensemble
Plus nous sommes ensemble
Plus heureux nous serons
Parce que tes amis sont mes amis
Et mes amis sont tes amis
Plus nous sommes ensemble
Plus heureux nous serons.

The More We Get Together
The more we get together, together, together
The more we get together
The happier we'll be
For your friends are my friends
And my friends are your friends
The more we get together
The happier we'll be.

quatre

4

Bonjour.
Je m'appelle Marie.
Comment t'appelles-tu?

Voici ma famille.

Hello.
My name is Marie.
What is your name?

Here is my family.

mon frère

mon père

ma mère

moi

My father
My mother
My brother
Me

Mon chat.
Il s'appelle Minou.
Il est gris.

My cat.
His name is Minou.
He is gray.

mon chat

Mon chien.
Il s'appelle Médor.
Il est noir et blanc.

mon chien

My dog.
His name is Médor.
He is black and white.

Here is my house.
My house has a brown
roof and a garden
with yellow flowers.

Ma chambre est bleue.
Il est sept heures.
Réveille-toi!
Réveille-toi!

My room is blue.
It is seven o'clock.
Get up!
Get up!

Alouette
Alouette, gentille alouette
Alouette, je te plumerai
Je te plumerai le bec
Je te plumerai le bec
Et le bec, alouette.

The Lark
Lark, oh lovely lark
Lark, I will pluck you now
I will pluck your little beak
I will pluck your little beak
And your beak, and your beak.

Frère Jacques
Frère Jacques, Frère Jacques
Dormez-vous, dormez-vous
Sonnez les matines
Sonnez les matines.
Ding dang dong!
Ding dang dong!

Are You Sleeping
Are you sleeping, are you sleeping
Brother John, Brother John
Morning bells are ringing
Morning bells are ringing.
Ding dang dong!
Ding dang dong!

neuf

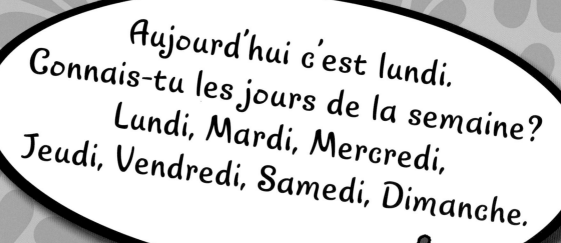

Today is Monday.
Do you know the days of the week?
Monday, Tuesday, Wednesday,
Thursday, Friday, Saturday, Sunday.

LUNDI
Monday

MARDI
Tuesday

MERCREDI
Wednesday

JEUDI
Thursday

VENDREDI
Friday

SAMEDI
Saturday

DIMANCHE
Sunday

Je m'habille. Je mets ma chemise, mon pantalon, mes chaussures et mon chapeau.

I get dressed. I put on my shirt, my pants, my shoes and my hat.

Tête, épaules, genoux et pieds

Tête, épaules, genoux et pieds, genoux et pieds
Tête, épaules, genoux et pieds, genoux et pieds
J'ai deux yeux, un nez, une bouche et deux oreilles
Tête, épaules, genoux et pieds, genoux et pieds.

Head, Shoulders, Knees and Toes
Head and shoulders, knees and toes, knees and toes
Head and shoulders, knees and toes, knees and toes
Eyes and ears and mouth and nose
Head and shoulders, knees and toes, knees and toes.

I eat breakfast.
I like bread and hot chocolate.

The weather is bad. It is raining.
I cannot go for a walk today.

Rain Medley

Rain, rain, go away
Come again another day
Rain, rain, go away
Little Johnny wants to play.

It's raining, it's pouring
The old man is snoring
He bumped his head and went to bed
And couldn't get up in the morning.

Pluie, pluie va-t-en

Pluie, pluie va-t-en
Reviens un autre jour
Petit Jean veut jouer
Pluie, pluie va-t-en.

Les arcs en ciel

Parfois bleu et parfois vert
Les couleurs les plus jolies
Que j'ai jamais vues
Rose et mauve, jaune – oui!
J'aime me balancer
Sous ces arcs en ciel.

Rainbows

Sometimes blue and sometimes green
Prettiest colors I've ever seen
Pink and purple, yellow - whee!
I love to ride those rainbows.

Voici mon école. Je dis, «Bonjour, maîtresse.» Je répète mes nombres et mon alphabet.

mon école

Here is my school.
I say, "Good morning, teacher."
I repeat my numbers
and my alphabet.

Les nombres

1	2	3	4	5	6	7	8	9	10
un	deux	trois	quatre	cinq	six	sept	huit	neuf	dix

Numbers

one two three four five six seven eight nine ten

L'ALPHABET

A a (ah)   B b (bay)   C c (say)   D d (day)

E e (er)   F f (effe)   G g (zhay)   H h (ahsh)   I i (ee)

J j (zheeh)   K k (kah)   L l (elle)   M m (emme)   N n (enne)

O o (oh)   P p (pay)   Q q (koo)   R r (air)   S s (esse)   T t (tay)

U u (oo) V v (vay) W w (doobluh vay) X x (eeks) Y y (ee grek) Z z (zed)

Maintenant je connais mon alphabet, la prochaine fois chanteras-tu avec moi?

Alphabet

A B C D E F G H
I J K L M N O P Q
R S T U V W X Y Z

Now I know my ABC's, next time won't you sing with me?

Marie avait un petit agneau

Marie avait un petit agneau, petit agneau, petit agneau
Marie avait un petit agneau, d'une teinte de neige pure
Et n'importe où Marie flânait, Marie flânait, Marie flânait
Et n'importe où Marie flânait, l'agneau suivait pour sûr.

Mary Had a Little Lamb

Mary had a little lamb, little lamb, little lamb
Mary had a little lamb, its fleece was white as snow
Everywhere that Mary went, Mary went, Mary went
Everywhere that Mary went the lamb was sure to go.

Un éléphant
Deux éléphants allaient jouer
Sur une toile d'araignée
Ils s'amusaient tellement bien
Qu'ils appelaient un autre, viens!

Deux...
Trois...
Quatre...
Tous...

One Elephant
One elephant went out to play
Upon a spider's web one day
He had such enormous fun
That he called for another elephant to come.

Two...
Three...
Four...
All...

Ainsi font

Ainsi font, font, font
Les petites marionettes
Ainsi font, font, font
Trois petits tours
Et puis s'en vont.

The Marionettes

This is what they do
What the marionettes do
What they do
What they do, do, do
Three turns round and they're
Through, through, through.

After school,
we drive in our car
to our house.

Les roues de la voiture

Les roues de la voiture tournent et tournent
Tournent et tournent, tournent et tournent
Les roues de la voiture tournent et tournent
Partout dans la ville.

Le klaxon de la voiture fait bip bip bip
Bip bip bip, bip bip bip
Le klaxon de la voiture fait bip bip bip
Partout dans la ville.

Les enfants dans la voiture disent
«Allons manger, allons manger
Allons manger»
Les enfants dans la voiture disent
«Allons manger»
Partout dans la ville.

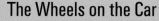

The Wheels on the Car

The wheels on the car go round and round
Round and round, round and round
The wheels on the car go round and round
All around the town.

The horn on the car goes beep beep beep
Beep beep beep, beep beep beep
The horn on the car goes beep beep beep
All around the town.

The children in the car go
"Let's have lunch, let's have lunch
Let's have lunch"
The children in the car go
"Let's have lunch"
All around the town.

C'est l'heure du déjeuner. Après le déjeuner, c'est la sieste.

It is lunch time.
After lunch it is nap time.

Dodo gentil bébé

Dodo gentil bébé dors en silence
Papa est parti t'acheter un canari
Si ce canari ne chante pas
Papa t'achètera une bague en diamant
Si ce diamant ne brille pas
Papa t'achètera un beau miroir doré
Si ce miroir se brise
Papa t'achètera une jolie petite chèvre.

Hush Little Baby

Hush little baby don't say a word
Papa's going to buy you a mockingbird
If that mockingbird won't sing
Papa's going to buy you a diamond ring
If that diamond ring turns brass
Papa's going to buy you a looking glass
If that looking glass falls down
You'll still be the sweetest little baby in town.

Après la sieste, nous allons au parc. Je vois les canards. Je chante, je danse sur le pont avec mes amis.

After our naps, we go to the park. I see the ducks. I sing, I dance on the bridge with my friends.

Sur le pont d'Avignon

Sur le pont, d'Avignon
L'on y danse, l'on y danse
Sur le pont, d'Avignon
L'on y danse tout en rond.

On the Bridge of Avignon
On the bridge of Avignon
They're all dancing, they're all dancing
On the bridge of Avignon
They're all dancing round and round.

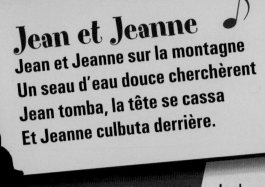

Jean et Jeanne

Jean et Jeanne sur la montagne
Un seau d'eau douce cherchèrent
Jean tomba, la tête se cassa
Et Jeanne culbuta derrière.

Jack and Jill
Jack and Jill went up the hill
To fetch a pail of water
Jack fell down and broke his crown
And Jill came tumbling after.

Six petits canards

Six petits canards que je connaissais
Des gros, des minces, des jolis, aussi
Mais un petit canard avec une plume sur le dos
Il guidait les autres avec son coin coin coin
Coin coin coin, coin coin coin
Il guidait les autres avec son coin coin coin.

Six Little Ducks
Six little ducks that I once knew
Fat ones, skinny ones, fair ones, too
But the one little duck with the feather on his back
He led the others with his quack quack quack
Quack quack quack, quack quack quack
He led the others with his quack quack quack.

Y'a un rat

Y'a un rat, dans le grenier, j'entends le chat qui miaule
Y'a un rat, dans le grenier, j'entends le chat miauler
J'entends, j'entends, j'entends le chat qui miaule
J'entends, j'entends, j'entends le chat miauler.

There's a Rat

There's a rat, in the attic, I hear the cat who's meowing
There's a rat, in the attic, I hear the cat meowing
I hear, I hear, I hear the cat who's meowing
I hear, I hear, I hear the cat meowing.

J'ai faim.
C'est l'heure du dîner.

I am hungry.
It is time for dinner.

Oh! Susanna

J'arrive tout droit de l'Alabama
Avec mon banjo sous le bras
Je vais comme ça vers la Louisiane
Pour retrouver ma Susanna
Oh! Susanna, ne pleure pas pour moi
J'arrive tout droit de l'Alabama
Avec mon banjo sous le bras.

Oh! Susanna
Well, I come from Alabama
With a banjo on my knee
I'm goin' to Louisiana my true love for to see
Oh, Susanna, won't you cry for me
'Cause I come from Alabama
With a banjo on my knee.

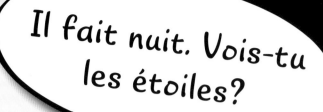

Il fait nuit. Vois-tu les étoiles?

It is night time.
Do you see the stars?

Ah! vous dirai-je Maman

Ah! vous dirai-je Maman
Ce qui cause mon tourment?
Papa veut que je raisonne
Comme une grande personne
Moi, je dis que les bonbons
Valent mieux que la raison.

Note: "Ah! vous dirai-je Maman" is a traditional French song to the tune of "Twinkle, Twinkle".

Twinkle, Twinkle

Twinkle, twinkle, little star
How I wonder what you are
Up above the world so high
Like a diamond in the sky
Twinkle, twinkle, little star
How I wonder what you are.

Fais dodo, Colas

Fais dodo, Colas, mon petit frère
Fais dodo, t'auras du lolo
Mama est en haut, qui fait du gâteau
Papa est en bas, qui fait du chocolat
Fais dodo, Colas, mon petit frère
Fais dodo, t'auras du lolo.

Go to Sleep, Colas

Go to sleep, Colas, my little brother
Go to sleep and you'll have a treat
Mama is upstairs making cakes
Papa is downstairs making chocolate
Go to sleep, Colas, my little brother
Go to sleep and you'll have a treat.

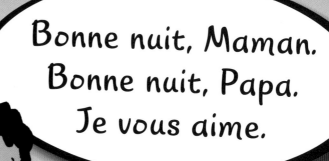

Goodnight, Mommy.
Goodnight, Daddy.
I love you.

Bonsoir mes amis

Bonsoir, mes amis, bonsoir
Bonsoir, mes amis, bonsoir
Bonsoir, mes amis
Bonsoir, mes amis
Bonsoir, mes amis, bonsoir.

Goodnight My Friends
Goodnight, my friends, goodnight
Goodnight, my friends, goodnight
Goodnight, my friends
Goodnight, my friends
Goodnight, my friends, goodnight.

Vous voulez en savoir plus?
(Want to learn more?)

la lampe

le banjo

le divan

la balle

le chien

l'oreiller

la fenêtre

le lit

la poupée

le chocolate chaud

le jus d'orange

le pain

la confiture

l'arbre

l'ami

le pont

de foot

les couleurs

rouge

violet

bleu

orange

vert

jaune

gris

marron

rose

blanc

noir